AROUND CORSHAM AND BOX

IN OLD PHOTOGRAPHS

CHURCH STREET from the gates of the church of St Bartholomew. Ethelred the Unready had a hunting lodge opposite the house pictured on the right, which is named Ethelred House. The houses on the left-hand side have the bale-shaped hoods for porches, which are indicative of a wool merchant's house. Note the old bracket lamp. This photograph was taken by Dr Eagles.

AROUND CORSHAM AND BOX IN OLD PHOTOGRAPHS

COLLECTED BY
ANNETTE WILSON AND
MIKE WILSON

ALAN SUTTON

Alan Sutton Publishing Limited
Phoenix Mill · Far Thrupp · Stroud · Gloucestershire

First published 1990

British Library Cataloguing in Publication Data

Around Corsham and Box in old photographs
1. Wiltshire, Corsham, 1900–1945 2. Wiltshire, Box, to 1984
I. Wilson, Annette *1932–* II. Wilson, Mike *1953–*
942.321

ISBN 0-86299-894-8

DEDICATION

Before he died in 1989, Tony Bishop of Bristol encouraged me to 'do another book', so here it is! A small token of thanks for his great friendship. I still laugh at some of his funny ways, and only wish he could have enjoyed the memories of Corsham and Box with us.

Typeset in 9/10 Korinna.
Typesetting and origination by
Alan Sutton Publishing Limited.
Printed in Great Britain by
The Bath Press, Avon.

CONTENTS

MR NICHOLAS STONEMAN-MERRET AND HIS WIFE FLORENCE outside their bungalow at Boxfields. Mr Merret was born in Cornwall in 1889, son of a Cornish tin miner, but moved to South Wales where he worked for thirty years as a coal miner. Mrs Merret was born in Gloucester in 1898, and apprenticed to Jolly's of Bath, as a seamstress. On coming to live in Box she became Chairman of Box Highlands School Governors, a member of Box Parish Council and a Councillor for Calne and Chippenham District. Mrs Merret's reputation as a very active member of the community is remembered today, even though she died in 1973. Behind Mr and Mrs Merret is an example of the bungalow accommodation which was erected at Boxfields during the war. None of these places exist now. On their demolition the sites became open quarries.

INTRODUCTION

Having compiled a book of photographs of Dursley and its surrounding villages with David Evans, while living in Slimbridge in Gloucestershire, it seemed only natural to collect pictures of my home town of Corsham, when I returned to Wiltshire after nineteen years.

With my son Mike press-ganged into doing the photography, we began on our collection, not just of Corsham pictures, but also of Box. This was a little daunting, as Box is not a territory with which we are very familiar, but as you will see when you read through, the response from the people of Box was one of great interest.

We are most grateful to everyone who has helped us with this project; even those with no photographs to offer have given names of people and places and stories about the photographs that we already had in our possession, giving us the essence of the life in the towns, rather than an idea of just the buildings. Most of the information that we have used was given to us by the contributors of the pictures, and we have tried to ensure that it is correct. Naturally, we have to allow for the failure of human memory, and the fact that the information has been given to us one or two generations on, which is why dates are sometimes stated as 'around'. We would be pleased to hear from anyone who can supplement the information that we have with names, dates, locations or anecdotes. We must apologize to anyone whose pictures have not been used, but the response to our request for photographs has been most gratifying, and in fact we are receiving invitations almost daily to go and see more material. Maybe at a future date we could do a second volume of Corsham and Box, as there is a wealth of history encapsulated in photographs of this area, which must be an ongoing source of interest, and Mike especially is appalled at the thought that some lovely old photographs could otherwise be lost forever.

We would like to express our gratitude to Kay Wilson for typing out the text, and to Jenny Harris for taking over whenever Kay was not available. Mike and I hope that this collection of photographs will bring great enjoyment to those of you who remember Corsham and Box as they were, and a sense of their history to the newcomers to the towns, and that seeing again some of the great characters and occasions of the past will evoke feelings of nostalgia.

Annette Wilson
Mike Wilson
Chippenham

THE AVENUE, CORSHAM PARK, taken from Corsham Court gates, before the fence and gates were erected.

Corsham and Box

In the days of the Saxon kings, Corsham was a royal manor. It is on record that Ethelred the Unready, who was King of Wessex from 978 until 1017, had a country palace here. It belonged to a son of Earl Godwin, William the Conqueror claimed it, and later the manor of Corsham was granted to John 'Lackland' by his brother Richard I. It was given to Richard Plantaganet, but he lost it when he supported the barons against the king. It was later given back to him by Henry II. In 1300 the manor was back in the possession of the king, who gave it to his daughter Mary, a nun, its value then being £97 a year. It passed to the sons and daughters of many kings and queens throughout the centuries, and because of this connection, was known as Corsham Regis. In 1777 an Act of Parliament authorized the sale of the manor to Mr Methuen.

The name Box probably comes from the name of the small tree or shrub which may have been introduced by the Romans, along with apple trees (Mallus) and other plants that we now consider to be native to Britain.

Box is sited in an advantageous position, especially for its ancient trades associated with the woollen industry such as clothiers, spinners, weavers, dyers, fullers, shearers and corders; the river supplied the power for the mills as well as for the milling of local grain. Old names like Box Mill Lane and Splatt Mill are among several reminders of the many mills that worked throughout the Avon valley.

Also important in its history is the stone industry. Quarrying into the surrounding hills provided the creamy coloured Oolite stone, which then gave work to builders of all trades. Most of the local buildings are made of this stone.

SECTION ONE

Schools and Children

CORSHAM ELEMENTARY SCHOOL was built in 1895 to accommodate 250 boys and 150 infants. The first headmaster was Mr Charles W. Churchill, after whom Churchill Avenue in Corsham was named. Left to right, standing: Harry Bond, -?-, Mr Alfred Jordan (headmaster), Ethel Hulbert, -?-, -?-, -?-, Madge Shillaker, -?-. Sitting: Don Osborne, Cecil Tanner, Jack Riddle, -?-, ? Conroy, -?-, -?-, -?-, Dorothy Head, Bertram Harris, Tom Hayward, Bunter Harris, -?-, -?-, Violet Whittle, Bob Prior, Arthur Hulbert, Charles Hampton, Kerwin Tucker, Eunice Merrett.

MR JORDAN, HEADMASTER, with the boys of Corsham Council School.

CORSHAM COUNCIL SCHOOL, 1949/50. Back row, left to right: Christine Arthand, Brenda Bowyer, Jean Clifford, Margaret Sewell, Carol Smith, Daphne Jones, Pamela Jones, Pauline Hale. Centre row, standing: -?-, ? Cole, Michael Cox, Michael Marshall, Ryan Laney, Henry Bird, -?-, Chris Osborne, -?-, Brian ?. Centre row, sitting: -?-, Barbara ?, Valerie Hayward, Mr Jones, -?-, -?-, Sylvia Hayes. Front row: ? Nash, -?-, -?-, ? Norris, -?-, -?-, -?-, Mervyn Hulbert.

THE REGIS SCHOOL. Mr Pearce, headmaster, and Mr Williams, form master.

MISS O'BRIEN WITH THE CHILDREN OF HER CLASS in 1963/4. Back row, left to right: -?-, Jeanette Morse, Sandra Hill, -?-, -?-, -?-, Timothy Hoare, Miss O'Brien, ?-, Robin Gold, Janet Brown, Elspeth Reed, Norma Changty. Middle row: Christine Baker, Stella Harris, Jenny Wilson, Pamela Witts, -?-, Glynis ?, Jane Holloway, -?-, -?-, -?-. Front row: -?-, -?-, Colin Seviour, Frankie Broom, -?-, Diane Brooks, Lorraine Merrit, -?-, Justine Walker, Una Biggs, -?-, -?-.

THE NATIVITY PLAY at Miss Bailey's Preparatory School in the High Street, Corsham, Christmas 1944. Back row, left to right: -?-, -?-, Poppy Bailey, -?-, -?-, Angela ?, Mary ?, Miss Bailey, -?-, Mrs Bebbington. Middle row, left to right: -?-, -?-, Michael Shorten, Maxwell Salmon, Stella Carter, Jean Pullen, Richard Bebbington, -?-, Judith ?, Peter Shorten, Malcolm Farleigh, Derek Farleigh. Front row, left to right: Marion ?, John Brown, -?-, Valerie Jacobs, Marion Farleigh, -?-, Monica and Mary ? (twins), Irene Taylor, Josephine Rossiter.

MAY FESTIVAL COUNTRY DANCERS from the Congregational Sunday school. Back row, left to right: Mary Edwards, Audrey Tucker, Audrey Reed, Jean Batley, Audrey Davis. Second row: Beatrice Davis, Joan Davis, Beatrice Salter, Diane Smith. Front row: ? Aust, Patricia Davis, Joyce Pullen, Audrey Davis.

FAIRIES AT THE FESTIVAL. Margaret Lewis, Jean Davies, Olive Davis (centre), Glenys Phillips (kneeling), Barbara Farmer (bowed).

HERALDS AT THE FESTIVAL. Gilbert Smith (herald), and attendants Haydon Brooks, Brian Ludlow, Arthur Davis and Joe Davies processed from Post Office Lane, through the High Street, down Church Street, along the Park Avenue, to Lacock Road, left to the Methuen Arms, and back down the High Street. The Herald was allowed on to the balcony of the Town Hall, to announce the arrival of the May Queen. Lady Methuen crowned the May Queen. She curtsied to 'Her Majesty' during the ceremony as the May Queen takes precedence over everyone on that day!

THE CHRISTMAS PLAY at the Regis School in 1964. Susan Boobyer was the Princess.

A DAY IN CORSHAM PARK in the summer of 1939. Louise Arthand and her daughter Pamela, who was born at Corsham Maternity Home on 3 March 1939.

SCOUT AND GUIDE CHRISTMAS PARTY 1953. Mrs Box, Guide Leader of 1st Corsham Guides, seated on the left; Derek Love, Scout Leader, 1st Corsham Scouts; Olwen Perry, Lieutenant 1st Corsham Guides, right.

JULIA TAYLOR WITH HER BROTHER TOM in the perambulator in the gardens of Easton Farm, 1920.

JULIA TAYLOR ON THE DONKEY with her brother Tom and Janet King from Minety Farm. The anvil to the right was in constant use for shoeing the farm horses.

CONGREGATIONAL SUNDAY SCHOOL AT WEAVERN in 1937/8. Nearby at Widdenham, the strict Baptists used the river for their baptisms in earlier times. From the left: Audrey Tucker, Diane Smith, Joyce Pullen, Jean Batley, Audrey and Pat Davis, Dora ?, and Audrey Davis.

BERNARD, MARLENE AND CONSTANCE, who came from London as evacuees on 2 September 1939, to live with Mrs Jones and daughters in Pickwick Road. This picture was taken at Weavern.

MIKE WILSON WITH HIS TRIANG ENGINE at Hudswell Lane. In the background is the power station of Basil Hill Barracks, on the far side of the Minnis sports ground. The power station provided heating for Basil Hill Barracks and the underground ammunition 'dump'. At the power station an electrically driven automatic grab travelled along the overhead track, picked up the coal and fed it into a hopper, which carried it to another hopper inside the boiler house. This fuel was mechanically fed into the furnace. Mr LenThomas was in charge of his shift, and worked there for about fifteen years.

CHILDREN of the members of the Royal Antediluvian Order of Buffaloes, Duke of Edinburgh Lodge, at a Christmas party at the Royal Oak in 1958/9. Mike Wilson is third from the left.

MARION GORDON-FARLEIGH AS THE OVALTINE MAID, in the fancy dress competition at Corsham cricket field in 1953, at the coronation carnival.

RICHARD BALL (right), AND SANDRA FORD, entrants in the fancy dress competition at the summer fête held at Box House, the home of the Hon. Mr and Mrs Shaw-Mellor.

PUPILS OF BOX SCHOOL on St George's Day, 1925 or '26. Standing, left to right: Ernie Rogers, Joan Wilkins, Vernon Taylor, -?-, Toby Smith, -?-, Ralph Reeves, Alec Cogswell, Kathleen Stinchcombe. Seated: -?-, -?-, Doris Gibbons, Dorothy Allen, -?-, Belinda Cousins, -?-, ? -?-. Some of the children are wearing roses, and some have handmade Union Jacks.

BOX CHURCH OF ENGLAND SCHOOL 1955/6. Some of the dignitaries present are: Mr Swan, schoolteacher; Mr Druett, headmaster; The Hon. Mrs Shaw-Mellor and Mr Oatley.

CHAPEL KNAPP CHURCH OF ENGLAND SCHOOL, 1960. To the left of the teacher is Barbara Martin. Peter Sedgwick is on the right of the front row and Richard Fowler third from the right.

SPORTS DAY AT BOX CHURCH SCHOOL.

PHYLLIS CURRANT AND REVD FOSTER'S TWO DAUGHTERS ZOE AND BETTY in the gardens at Box Vicarage.

GASTARD SCHOOL GARDENING CONTINGENT.

GASTARD SCHOOL, CHAPEL KNAPP. Mr and Mrs Foreword were headmaster and mistress.

CHAPEL KNAPP SCHOOL, Gastard, 1903. The headmaster was Mr Foreword.

BOX SCHOOL c. 1952. The teacher is Bert Swan.

CHILDREN'S FLOWER SHOW at Gastard in 1929. Wild flowers were arranged by the children themselves with prizes given by their parents – sweets, little cakes or similar goodies. Back row, left to right: Frankie Merrett, Joyce Kelly, Nancy Grey, Leonard Simmons. Front row, left to right: Gladys Gray, Barbara Fowler, Betty Shepherd, Nellie Gray.

LEONARD, KATHLEEN AND GODREY MARTIN, the children of the landlord of the Harp and Crown, Gastard, 1921.

MARY ELIZABETH GLADYS BARNETT AND HER BROTHER BILLY, 1917. They lived at Seven Stars, Gastard, where their family had a grocery shop.

NELLY AND BARBARA FOWLER in the Drung at Gastard. Drung is a name for an alley between the houses.

ATWORTH SCHOOL, 1920. Vera Sheppard is the first right in the middle row. The headmaster at this time was Mr Inkpen.

SECTION TWO

People

SIR SEYMOUR HOWARD OF COURTLANDS, Lacock Road, Corsham, who became Lord Mayor of London in 1954.

SIR EDWARD HOWARD OF COURTLANDS, Lacock Road, Corsham, who became Lord Mayor of London. His father had held this office ten years before.

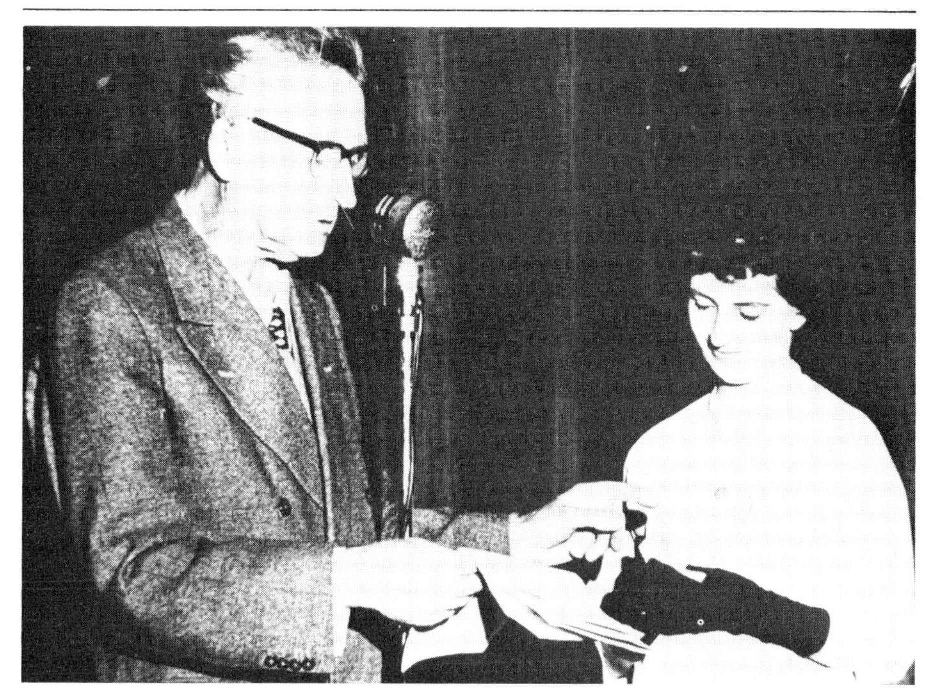

LORD METHUEN presenting Annette Wilson with a cheque for £1,000 at Bath Odeon in 1965. This was the prize for a competition in *Woman's Weekly*, choosing suitable wedding gifts for a newly married couple.

MR HEZEKIAH HANCOCK was born in 1874, one of a long line of Hancocks whose family can be traced back in this area for centuries. Farmers, carriers and coal merchants are some of the businesses in which the family have been, and still are, involved. Hancock's the Coal Merchants is still run by his grandson Clive and granddaughter Joyce.

THE REVD HAROLD JONES CLEANING THE LAUNDRY CHIMNEY for Mrs Hale, who was unable to light her boiler and get on with her work as a laundress.

THE REVD HAROLD JONES, his wife, daughter Doreen and Kim, the wire haired terrier. Mr Jones came to Corsham in 1934 and, until his death in 1938, the chapels in his care included the Congregational Church, Pickwick Road, Corsham Monk's Chapel and Chapel Knapp, Gastard. He also preached at Lacock.

MISS LIGHT AND MISS GOULD in their garden at Prospect with their pets: a tabby cat, a guinea pig and three tortoises, one of whom was called Bluebell. Tortoises are now a valuable possession as they may no longer be imported.

MRS HALE, HER SON AND DAUGHTER-IN-LAW AND THEIR FOUR CHILDREN in the field at the end of Providence Lane. Mrs Hale, a laundress, had her laundry in Providence Lane.

WILLIAM BEER at the back door of the Brewery. William, the son of the licensee of the Red Lion, Lacock, became the publican of the Brewery, Priory Street, Corsham in 1924. His wife, Elizabeth Gainey, came from Langley Burrell. They lived at the Brewery for thirty-two years, until William's death.

MRS ELIZABETH (BETTY) BEER at the horse trough at the junction of Priory Street and High Street, Corsham. This photograph, taken in 1925, shows a veritable lady of fashion – narrow brimmed, high crowned hat, mid-calf-length coat and pointed-toed shoes.

MR NEAL, who started the brushworks in Pickwick Road in 1811. It was burnt down on 20 May 1921. It was then rebuilt and work continued until it closed in the early 1960s.

VERA ROSSITER, who became a sister at Southmead Hospital, Bristol, and Chippenham District Hospital. This photograph was taken while at nursing college when she was twenty-three years old.

MR WILLIAM BEARD with his wife and five daughters. Seated to his left is Evelyn and standing behind them, from left to right, are Florence, Hilda, Elsie and Annie. Evelyn married Walter Sheppard, manager of the Bradford Road Quarry.

MR HENRY GOUGH WITH HIS WIFE LOUISA and children Ivy, Alan and Ruby. Mr Gough, a builder, came from Calne. Ruby married Herbert Edwards on 15 May 1923 at the Methodist church, Pickwick Road, Corsham.

CYRIL AND PERCY BADMINTON in around 1921.

ELIZABETH AND VERA ROSSITER, who lived at Ashford Cottage, Priory Street in 1903.

NORAH HANCOCK AND HER SISTER GERTRUDE LODGE with Gertrude's children Gwendolin, John and Dorothy, at their home in Potley Lane, around 1930.

MISS BETTY WOOD, whose family owned the Paul Street glove factory. Miss Wood continued to run the business after her father's death.

CHRISTINE ARTHAND, Air Officer Commanding's secretary, in the archway at Rudloe Manor, Fighter Command.

A GROUP OF BOX GENTLEMEN outside the Northey Arms. From left to right: Harry Horsell, George Currant, Bill Peadon, -?-, George Shepherd, --?-, -?-, -?-, -?-, Frank Ford, Albert Tye.

MR FRANK GITTINGS, the shepherd, and his wife at Farm Cottage, Ashley.

MR AND MRS GEORGE CURRANT with Winnie and Effie, the older of their eleven children, at the door of their cottage at Ashley, Box in 1904.

GEORGE HANCOCK AND HIS WIFE ALICE with their daughters Phyllis and Joyce, 1913. Mr Hancock was a quarryman but during the war, because he was disabled, he worked at the Melksham rubber works. At the end of the war he returned to the quarries.

FLORENCE COGSWELL, centre, with her children, Win and Ted.

MR GEORGE AND MRS ALICE HANCOCK with their six daughters in 1925. From left to right: Laura, Evelyn, Joyce (behind her father), Phyllis (behind her mother), Gwendoline and Doris. Mrs Hancock died soon after this photograph was taken.

ANNIE MARIA CLIFFORD, daughter of Mrs Fletcher, post lady of Box and Colerne, who lived in a cottage at Mills Platt with her children. From left to right: Lily Rosina Ivy, born 1899, died aged eleven or twelve; Arthur Henry, born 1902; Eveline Ethel, born 1885, and Reginald Percival, born 1909.

MRS AGNES BALL with her children Anne and Richard, and friends outside Hazelbury Cottage, 1962.

MR ELI SHEPPARD OF ATWORTH, who lived in Church Street and died aged ninety-five.

ELLEN MAY, WHO BECAME MRS OATLEY. She lived in Bradford Road with her husband Samuel, who was a quarryman. They had six children.

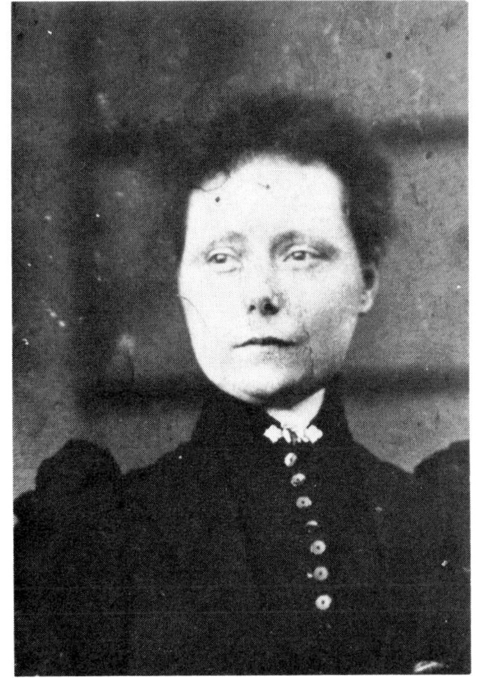

MARY ELIZABETH FIELDING of Gastard, who became the wife of Eli Barnett of Velley Hill. They lived at Seven Stars, Gastard.

MRS NELLIE FOWLER of Gastard, with her son Richard, 1916.

MR GILLSON LIVED ON HIS OWN AT SANDPITS FARM, Gastard. He went to fight in the First World War. On his return to his home, he knelt and thanked God, then he took his key from under the doormat, where it had lain throughout the war!

MEMBERS OF CHAPEL KNAPP FOOTBALL CLUB, 1936/7: Bert Porter, Fred Gray, Dick Fowler, Sid Hand, Len Simmons, ? Parson.

ON AN OUTING, in typical fashions of the time (1937): Brenda Scudamore, Nellie Gray, Mary Smith, Daphne Freegard, Eileen Hemming.

ARCHIBALD CARTER CAME HOME FROM SCHOOL at the age of six years, in around 1920, to be told that his mother was dead. Mrs Edith Carter of Easton, had gone to Easton Farm to help with the spring cleaning. She and another maid were cleaning the kitchen and had to take guns down from a shelf. Somehow Mrs Carter was shot, the only witness being the other maid. There was a long police investigation, and the jury returned a verdict of death from gunshot wounds, in an unexplained way.

MRS LODGE OUTSIDE HER HOUSE, Brockleaze Cottage, Corshamside, Neston. This picture was taken in the late 1930s.

SECTION THREE

Church and Chapel

ST BARTHOLOMEW'S PARISH CHURCH, Corsham, south-west view prior to 1874. The church is of Norman origin and was added to in Decorated and Perpendicular styles. It consists of a chancel with chapels, nave with five bays, aisles and a south chapel with tower and porch.

ST BARTHOLOMEW'S PARISH CHURCH, Corsham, west view. The spire with its six bells was added and the tower redesigned in approximately 1874. Lord Methuen added a chapel for himself and his family in 1897 and the carved stone screen in the south aisle and the choir vestry were added in 1930, under the direction of Sir Harold Brakspear, KCVO.

CORSHAM CHURCH. There is evidence of early Norman work in the parish church of St Bartholomew at Corsham. Restoration carried out in 1874 unfortunately destroyed a lot of interesting medieval work. Note the ivy on the tower.

THE WEDDING OF HENRY EDWARD POCOCK AND LILIAN ESTHER KING at Corsham church in 1914. Nurses of the Voluntary Aid Detachment (VAD) formed the Guard of Honour. Mr and Mrs Pocock are the parents of Mrs Eagles.

CORSHAM CHURCH CHOIR sang at many venues, one being the wedding of Miss Lysley at Castle Combe. Field Marshall Lord Methuen was a guest at the wedding. Later in the week he met Mr Lewin Spackman in Corsham High Street, and said 'Spackman, you'll have to look to your laurels'.

'Why is that m'Lord.'

'I went to a wedding in Castle Combe and they've got a choir as good as, if not better than yours.'

'It was mine, m'Lord' said Mr Spackman.

Corsham Church Choir 1924. Back row left to right: Fred Knott, Herbert Edwards, George Mallard, Ron Barnett. Second row: Harold Moody, Harry Lakeman, Alfred Bird, Olive Holloway, Olivia Butler, Mary Carter, -?-, William Dunning, Arthur Hampton. Seated: Lewin Spackman (choirmaster), -?-, -?-, -?-, -?-, the Revd Clark, Fred Mallard, -?-, -?-, Fred Reeves, -?-. -?-, -?- Roy Henstridge, Charles Hampton, -?-.

THE WEDDING OF JOHN COURT AND PAMELA ARTHAND. John taught at Corsham Secondary Modern School before moving to Durham to continue his career in psychology.

MR LEON ARTHAND, organist at St Patrick's Roman Catholic church, with new electronic organ, installed in 1964/5 to replace the old harmonium. This organ had a very short life. The fumes from the central heating system had an adverse effect on the metal components!

A SOCIAL OCCASION at the hall of the Roman Catholic church, Pickwick. Originally this church was the Pickwick School, but with the influx of a large Catholic community during the Second World War, it was found necessary to have a proper church. Before being converted into a church, the building was used as a gas mask factory. Some of those in the picture are: standing, left to right: -?-, -?-, two children, Mrs Martin, Mrs Rusell, Mrs Ryan (?), Mrs Mary Hall. Seated, left to right: -?-, Father Supple (the Roman Catholic priest), Mr Leon Arthand (organist), Mr Tom Watson (sacristan).

MR A.J. HOBBS, CHIEF FIRE OFFICER, in charge of the Corsham fire-engine, which was being used as a bridal carriage. Mr Hobbs had a saddlery and cycle repair shop in the High Street.

A BRIDAL PARTY LEAVING THE METHODIST CHURCH, Pickwick Road, Corsham.

SUNDAY SCHOOL ANNIVERSARY FESTIVAL at the Congregational Church in Pickwick Road, 1940/1. The pulpit was removed to make room for the children's performance. This chapel is now used as a printing works.

THE MARRIAGE OF RUBY GOUGH AND HERBERT EDWARDS in Corsham at the Methodist church, 15 May 1923. Even the bride's shoes are flower-bedecked!

CONGREGATIONAL SUNDAY SCHOOL WALK TO WEAVERN. Pat Davis, Audrey Tucker, Jean Batley, Audrey Davis, Audrey Davis (a different family), Diana Smith, Joyce Pullen and Dora ?.

THE PULPIT AND PEWS IN THE CHAPEL OF THE WARDEN'S HOUSE, at the Hungerford Almshouses at the junction of Lacock Road and Pound Pill.

BOX METHODIST CHURCH AND HALL, which was opened around 1907.

ARMISTICE DAY SERVICE at Box cenotaph 1951. The vicar was the Reverend Lendon Bell.

THE WEDDING OF ALBERT COGSWELL TO FLORENCE ALICE at the parish church of Thomas á Becket, Box, 4 September 1904.

THE MARRIAGE OF DOUGLAS HANCOCK AND EFFIE CURRANT at the church of Thomas á Becket in Box, Christmas Eve, 1932. Effie is wearing a red dress and hat made for her by Colmers of Bath. She taught at Corsham School.

THE MARRIAGE OF HARRY ROSSITER AND MISS QUEENIE HAYWARD, who were married at Box parish church.

THE WEDDING OF GWENDOLINE HANCOCK AND DAVID GIBSON, which took place at Box Methodist church in 1945. On the left are: Mrs Pashley (bride's sister) and son Malcolm, and Mrs Evelyn Day (bride's sister). Mr Pashley is holding his daughter Maureen on the far right, and standing next to him is Mr Hancock (bride's father).

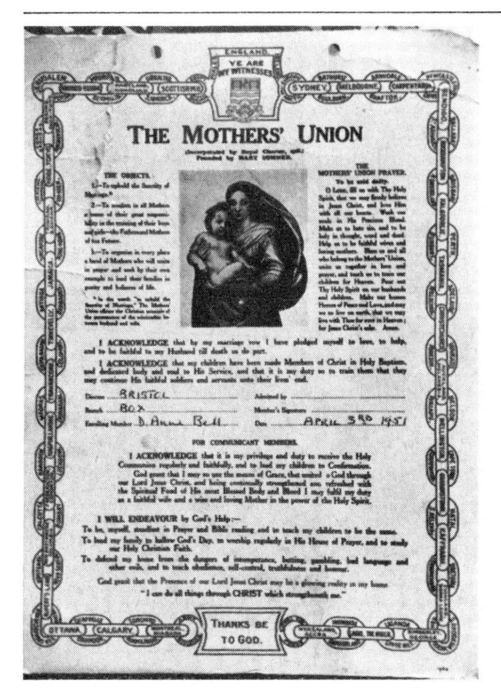

ENGLAND

YE ARE MY WITNESSES

SYDNEY

THE MOTHERS' UNION

I ACKNOWLEDGE that by my marriage vow I have pledged myself to love, to help, and to be faithful to my Husband till death us do part.

I ACKNOWLEDGE that my children have been made Members of Christ in Holy Baptism, and dedicated body and soul to His Service, and that it is my duty so to train them that they may continue His faithful soldiers and servants unto their lives' end.

Diocese BRISTOL

Branch BOX

Enrolling Member D. Anne Bell

Admitted by

Member's Signature

Date APRIL 5TH 1951

FOR COMMUNICANT MEMBERS.

I ACKNOWLEDGE that it is my privilege and duty to receive the Holy Communion regularly and faithfully, and to lead my children to Confirmation.

God grant that I may so use the means of Grace, that united to God through our Lord Jesus Christ, and being continually strengthened and refreshed with the Spiritual Food of His most Blessed Body and Blood I may fulfil my duty as a faithful wife and a wise and loving Mother in the power of the Holy Spirit.

I WILL ENDEAVOUR by God's Help:—

To be, myself, steadfast in Prayer and Bible reading and to teach my children to be the same.

To lead my family to hallow God's Day, to worship regularly in His House of Prayer, and to study our Holy Christian Faith.

To defend my home from the dangers of intemperance, betting, gambling, bad language and other evils, and to teach obedience, self-control, truthfulness and honour.

God grant that the Presence of our Lord Jesus Christ may be a glowing reality in my home.

"I can do all things through CHRIST which strengtheneth me."

OTTAWA CALGARY

THANKS BE TO GOD.

AN ENROLMENT CARD for members of the Mother's Union. This one belongs to Mrs Ball of Corsham.

MONK'S CHAPEL, built by the Quakers in the early part of the seventeenth century. Because of the distance travelled to the chapel early in its use, people would spend the whole day there. They would bring food and cook it over the fire which was used to heat the chapel.

THE PARISH CHURCH OF ST JOHN THE BAPTIST, Gastard, built in 1912.

AFTER THE MARRIAGE of Mary Barnett of Seven Stars, Gastard to Mr Godfrey Martin of the Harp and Crown, Gastard, 1936. Back row, left to right: Kathleen Martin, Sid Fletcher holding Mary, Mr Eli Barnett, Billy Barnett, Doris Fletcher. Front row: Mr and Mrs Frank Fielding, Mr Godfrey Martin (landlord of Harp and Crown), Mrs Barnett, Barbara Hayward, Brenda Sandaman, -?-, -?-, -?-.

BILLY BARNETT AND KATHLEEN HILL, after their marriage on 13 May 1940.

PARISH CHURCH OF ST PHILIP AND ST JAMES, Neston, opened 1 May 1866. Built in the Early English style with a chancel and nave and a turret with one bell. There are five stained-glass windows, presented by A.C. Mitchell Esq., in memory of his wife.

MUCH HAS BEEN WRITTEN ABOUT THE HISTORY OF CHAPEL PLAISTER which was in the parish of Hazelbury. Hazelbury, a very ancient parish, had a resident priest in the days of Edward the Confessor. There was once a parish church behind Hazelbury Manor, about three quarters of a mile from Chapel Plaister. It has been, in its time, a resting place for pilgrims to Glastonbury, an outhouse of an alehouse called The Bell, one of a pair of cottages, a chicken house and a store, until it was restored as a chapel in 1893.

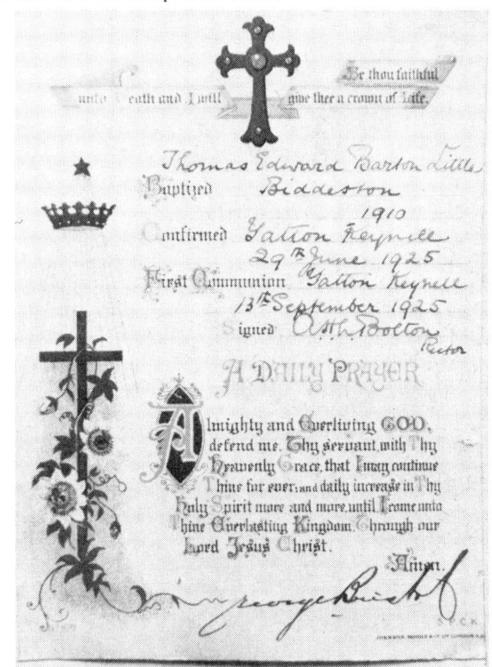

Be thou faithful unto Death and I will give thee a crown of Life.

Thomas Edward Barton Little

Baptized Biddeston 1910

Confirmed Yatton Keynell 29th June 1925

First Communion Yatton Keynell 13th September 1925

Signed A.H. Bolton Rector

A DAILY PRAYER

Almighty and Everliving GOD, defend me, Thy servant, with Thy Heavenly Grace, that I may continue Thine for ever; and daily increase in Thy Holy Spirit more and more, until I come unto Thine Everlasting Kingdom, through our Lord Jesus Christ. Amen.

THE CONFIRMATION CERTIFICATE OF MR T. LITTLE of Slaughterford. He was baptized at Biddestone in 1910 and was confirmed at Yatton Keynell in June 1925 by the Bishop of Bristol, and took his first communion on 13 September 1925.

THE ARCHBISHOP VINING'S CHURCH BOYS' CAMP, 1969. Front row, left to right: -?-, -?-, -?-, Mervyn Drewitt, Adrian Tipper, Peter ? (vicar of Ware), 'Spider' Hall (former Archbishop of West Africa).

SOME OF THE CAROL SINGERS from Toc H were, from left to right: D. Farmer, D. Jones, M. Sawbridge, Alison Jones, Cynthia Merrett, Effie Hancock, -?-, -?-, Pat ?, Des Harris (conducting), -?-, -?-, -?-, -?-, Bobby Mines, Percy Badminton, Jim Mines, Mr Bidmead, Keith and David Badminton, Mr Bevan and Joe James.

SECTION FOUR

Occupations

STATION ROAD STONEYARD. The manager was Herbert Head. Among the men pictured are Derek Andrews and George Tanner to the right of the back row. Mr Tanner was also a bell ringer. In the second row is Bill Pickett, left, in trilby hat; Arthur Newbury; Arthur Hulbert in the centre; Mr Lodge, wearing a white apron. In the front row, about fourth from the left, is Reggie Heaven.

THE WORKED STONEYARDS IN CORSHAM where the lovely local Oolitic limestone was fashioned into keystones, quoins, gable ends, porticoes, etc.

CORSHAM STONE WHARF, a very busy site at the height of the stone working era. The houses of The Cleeve are in the background, the fields are new completely built over. Large wild strawberries grew along the embankment during the summertime.

ELI BARNETT, QUARRYMAN, coming up from Monks Park Quarry with a party of officials from Bath.

MEN AT WORK IN MONKS PARK QUARRY. From left to right: ? Osborne, Jack ?, ? Brooks, Reginald Pashley. Mr Pashley worked with the horses in the quarry and would go back and forth to the stables in Bradford Road to bed them down and feed them.

THIS SAMSON CUTTER, being driven by J. Stannard at Moor Park Quarry, belonged to the Bath and Portland stone firms. This machine was first used in the coal mines and then converted for cutting stone in 1948.

SOME OF THE GIRLS WHO WORKED AT PAUL STREET GLOVE FACTORY, which was owned by Mr Woods. This picture was taken in 1935. All the girls pictured were makers, which meant that they made the complete glove apart from the thumb. Back row, left to right: Phyllis Trotman, Dorothy Pain, Nancy Moody, Lucy Fisher, Doris Gosling. Front row: Nellie Gray, Peggy Moody, Kath Phelps, Mary Cainey, Betty Potter, Monica Gale and Mary Smith.

CORSHAM GLOVE FACTORY, Paul Street, 1952, owned by the Wood family of Pickwick Road. From left to right: Gertie Hutchings, Pam Jones, Rose Wakeley, -?-, Gillian May, Ruby ?, Barbara Clifford, Carol Simpson, Mary Crowle, Sheila Green.

PAUL STREET GLOVE FACTORY, early 1950s. Standing, left to right: Sheila Sawyer, Irene Tilley, June Muzelle, Betty Ballen, Joan Green. Sitting: -?-, Maureen Kelly, Philomena South, Ruby ?

JOSEPH ROSSITER AND MR CLETHEROE, members of Corsham Voluntary Fire Brigade. They served when the fire-engine was a hand-driven machine. Photograph 1924.

MR H. BANKS WAS A FLY OPERATOR. He had the only hackney carriage business in Corsham. It was situated at the top of Station Road, adjacent to the cricket field. With the advent of the motor car, Mr Banks retired from the carriage business and became manager of the Royal Wilts. Pork Shop.

MR GAINEY OF LANGLEY BURRELL with his granddaughter Jean Philpott, standing in the back garden of his son-in-law's public house, the Brewery, Priory Street, Corsham. Mr Beer, the publican, made handcarts and barrows, and Mrs Beer would help with the painting of them. They would then be taken to be sold at Chippenham market. Mr Beer trained in this skill at Humphries Wagon Works, in London Road, Chippenham.

HAYMAKING IN SMITH'S MEADOW, on the Westrop side of Easton Farm. George Carter is receiving the load from the Massey Harris hay loader. Mrs M. Taylor, with daughter Vera, and friends are in the foreground. During a severe outbreak of foot and mouth disease at the end of the last century, Mr Taylor's grandfather and one of the carters took a broad-wheeled Wiltshire wagon loaded with cheese made at Easton Farm, to the market in Reading, as all markets locally were closed due to the infection. On the journey he had to remove the spreaders and use them to beat off the hungry citizens they met on the way who tried to steal the cheeses.

HAYMAKING AT EASTON FARM in the 1920s involved using a Cottise Sweep between two horses to gather the hay, in this instance at Brick Hill.

OSBORNE BUILDING CONTRACTORS WORKFORCE 1933. This photograph was taken in front of the barn in the yard of the Methuen Arms (note the pigeon lofts). Among those present were, from left to right, standing: Ted Say, painter; Fred Gale, chippy; Bob Langridge, plumber; Frank Fletcher; Alfred Reed; ? Fry; Lawrence Waite; William Young; -?-; Walter Baker; Jack Simmonds; Harry Simmonds; Mr Albert Osborne. Kneeling: Kenneth Lumkin; Jack Lumkin, chippy; Billy Brown, painter; Ernie Cole, joiner; Bill Taylor; Carl Buckle, driver; Stanley Osborne, carver of ornamental stone items. In the wagon, from the left: Arthur Newbury; Billy Hatter; Bob Wright, mason, Verdun Cole; Charles Hampton; Cecil Stilman, plumber. Standing, back: Walter Gingell; Bill Frankum; Ted Wooten; Bob Oatley; Ken Taylor; Arthur Gingell, mason; Frank Taylor, plasterer and tiler; Sam Gale, banker mason; Arthur Coleman, painter; George Cole, carpenter. Among the Osborne workers, joiners were nicknamed 'Silver Assed Carpenters' because of the white aprons they wore!

THE KINGS AVENUE ESTATE DURING CONSTRUCTION. Pre-fabricated bungalows, built as war time accommodation, were demolished and houses and flats were put up in their place. They were built by Calne and Chippenham Rural District Council for council tenants. (Looking toward Coulston Road.)

THE TEACHERS AT CORSHAM COUNCIL SCHOOL, 1946/7. Left to right, standing: Mr Morris, Mr Wellman, Mr Hart (headmaster), Mr Gray, Mr Steel. Seated: Miss Perry, Mrs Owen, Mrs Hancock, Mrs Weller, Mrs Buckingham.

AFTER DUNKIRK it was impossible to find a laundry to take the troops' washing, as it was so dirty after the men returned to Britain. Mrs Arthand organized the ladies of Potley Lane, and the washing was delivered to her house, where it was disinfected, boiled, and put into bundles, then delivered to the houses in the district. It was laundered for 10 d. a bundle, and when it had been washed and returned, Mrs Arthand repaired every garment and replaced any missing buttons. After the first wash, it was a straightforward delivery and laundry job, that continued until the men were posted to new destinations. The picture shows Christine Arthand bringing in a bundle of laundry – her cry was 'More washing Mum!'

THIS BEAUTIFUL DISPLAY is outside what is thought to be Abraham's butchers shop, in the early 1900s. This shop was situated in Pickwick Road, opposite the entrance to the Congregational chapel, the edge of the roof of which can just be seen on the extreme left of the picture.

H.R. JAMES' IRONMONGERY in the High Street, Corsham. Outside the shop are Mr H.R. James and his son Joseph.

OUTSIDE THE PLOUGH OFF LICENCE in the High Street. From the right: Mrs Simmons with her daughter Valerie, and Yvonne Jackson.

CORSHAM'S FIRST POSTMARK shown in the top right-hand corner, dated 1840. The dark patch on the lower portion is red sealing wax.

MRS FLETCHER FROM COLERNE became the post lady for Colerne and Box. In addition to delivering the mail, she had to walk to Corsham to collect the mail from the sorting office twice a day. She had a daughter Annie Maria who was born in 1856.

MR JOHN CLIFFORD, 1855–1919, of Calstone, Calne, who was the blacksmith for Bath and Portland Stone at the Cliff Quarry, Box. He married Annie Maria Fletcher at Chippenham in 1877, and they had a total of ten children.

ALBERT COGSWELL, MASTER MASON, at the Wharf Stoneyard, Box. Stone from Clift Quarry was taken down the tramway under the main road to the wharf, from where it was shipped out on Bath and Portland's own railway wagons.

MR RICHARD (DICK) FOWLER worked for the Bath and Portland Stone firm and for the Yockney and Hartham Park Stone Company. This company stayed independent until 1944.

IVOR BALL, SECOND GARDENER AT HAZELBURY MANOR, driving the mowing machine. His brother George was the garden boy, with David Dean of Chapel Plaister. Hazelbury Manor was then the home of Mr and Mrs George Kitsone. The late Mr Arthur Catterell, who grew up in Box, remembered going to Hazelbury Manor during the school holidays and being paid 3d. a day for digging daisies out of the lawn. He also remembered the Christmas parties given by the Hon. Mrs Shaw-Mellor for all the village schoolchildren. They were each given a quarter of a pound of chocolates. Mr Catterell became a banker mason for the Bath and Portland Stone firm. He worked on Buckingham Palace, repairing the war damage. He also worked on Eton College, Highgrove House and the chancel of Calne church.

MR AND MRS MATTHEWS OF ASHLEY FARM stop for a break. The cow in front of them is a Scottish beast with an unfriendly disposition. They were treating it for a ripped teat which it had stepped on and torn. Unfortunately, the cow was very uncooperative.

IVOR BALL MOVED FROM HAZLEBURY MANOR, Box, to be 'ornamental' gardener at Corsham Court in 1955. He is seen here clearing stumps from an old copse.

MR ELI BARNETT AND HIS SON BILLY painting the house at Seven Stars, Gastard.

STONE BEING LIFTED FROM AN OPEN QUARRY at South Wraxall. Mrs Vera Fowler, wife of Richard Fowler, quarryman, climbed down the wall across the quarry to take this snapshot!

ONE OF THE LARGE CRANES USED AT THINGLEY JUNCTION to load shipments of ammunition during the Second World War.

MR BILL FIELDING worked a smalholding at Thingley.

MR BRYANT AND MR HUMPHRIES resting from cutting the grass around Monk's Chapel.

MR SALMON, CHIEF CONSTABLE, presenting Mrs Northover with a bouquet and Mr Northover with a clock and a long service medal after over thirty years as a policeman.

WORKERS FROM NESTON GLOVE FACTORY enjoying an outing to Seaton, 1958. Back row, left to right: Phyllis Hancock; Sheila Romain, who was a glover; Margaret Elms, a thumber; Pat ?, fur-lining cutter; Brian Risbrook. Centre: Bill Hancock, cutter; Kitty Tight; Tony Poynting; -?-, ironer. Front row: Pat Earl and Pam Jones, brosser maker (a brosser was the gathering up of the wrist of a long glove). This factory was owned by a Mr and Mrs Moss, and the manager was Mr Allen.

MR AND MRS HANCOCK OF CORSHAMSIDE. Mr Hancock raised a few pigs each year for the family larder.

JOHN SAWYER AND HIS BROTHER WILLIAM preparing the (Ransome) skimmer which they used to skim the stubble from 'John's' field in Jaggards Lane in 1935. In a summer as hot as that of 1990 Mr Sawyer said the ground was so hard that he had had to ride the skimmer in order to add weight to the machine. Captain and Duke were the horses used for the job.

SECTION FIVE

Transport

CORSHAM RAILWAY STATION was on the GWR main line from Bristol to London. Note the change from gas to electric lighting which took place sometime during the 1950s.

CORSHAM RAILWAY STATION under flood in 1935. Note the floodwater pouring into the cutting over the wall by the waiting room on the left. Charles Lanham may still have been the station master as he was certainly in the post in 1939.

LOOKING FROM POTLEY BRIDGE TOWARD CORSHAM STATION. The 'bridge' was an aqueduct known by the local children as the 'ackydock'. The Station Road stoneyards are to the right, Station Hotel is in the middle distance, and the Cleeve to the right.

THE BOX END OF BOX TUNNEL, built for the GWR by Isambard Kingdom Brunel. This tunnel is one and three quarters of a mile long. Work on it was commenced in 1836 and completed in 1841.

FREDDY MARSH holds the horse, Len Marsh stands at the tail, outside the shop owned by their brother George Marsh. Fruit, vegetables and fish were sold in this shop in Pickwick Road, opposite the 'new' library.

MR H. BANKS, FLY OPERATOR, with one of his fly carriages. His hackney carriage business was situated at the top of Station Hill, adjacent to the cricket field. Mr Banks became manager of the Royal Wilts. Pork Shop when his business closed with the advent of the motor engine.

THIS COACH OUTING numbered the Rossiter family among its passengers. The charabanc was probably built at the Bristol Tramways & Carriage Co. They started to build motorbuses in 1906, mostly for journeys around the city. Their premises were at Filton but they moved from there when more space was needed to build Bristol aeroplanes.

THIS BEAUTIFUL CHARABANC, taking a party from Gastard on an outing, probably belonged to Hancocks, the carriers of Gastard. Note the iron wheels. Mrs Nellie Fowler is seated at the front of the bus.

PICKWICK ROAD, with the Methuen Arms in the background. The Jowitt in the foreground had a prototype engine which was later used in the Jowett Javelin before the Second World War.

MR L. ARTHAND'S FORD pictured at Hudswell. It had a windscreen that opened forward.

A 25 HP HUPMOBILE CAR, being used to pull a 1 hp float made by Humphries Wagon Works of Chippenham. Corn was hand flailed in this beautiful barn at Easton Farm.

MR H.J.H. TAYLOR'S HILLMAN TOURER, upside down at the Two Ponds, Easton crossroads, after being hit by another car and rolling into the pond. There were very few cars in the area at the time. Mr Harry Carter had to be rescued from under the hood by being pulled through the water. The bull-nosed Morris Oxford coupé belonged to a neighbour of the Taylors, and John Taylor was brought out to see the accident and is sitting in the dickie seat of the Morris. (Photograph taken in the late 1920s.)

A LINE-UP OF AMBULANCES on the Castle Combe race circuit, before taking up their positions on the track for first aid duty. Two ambulances from Corsham Division and one from Pressed Steel Division, Swindon. The ambulance crews were: J. Stannard, -?-, L. Johnson, J. Hancock, -?-, and L. Harris.

DICK FOWLER on his first motor cycle, a New Imperial, in 1927.

THE HANDING OVER OF THE KEYS of a new ambulance by Mrs Hancock and a representative from Walker Jackson of Swindon. This ambulance was partly paid for by a race meeting held at the Castle Combe circuit in aid of the St John Ambulance Brigade. From the left: B. Bates, J. Stannard, R. Crowle, B. Shillaker and Mrs Hancock.

MR ARTHAND ON HIS ARIEL MOTOR CYCLE, before enlisting in the Army in 1939. Having served with the 1st Battalion Royal Scots during and after the First World War, Mr Arthand, as a gunnery instructor, was stationed at 'The Dump' in the Royal Artillery.

MR AND MRS RICHARD FOWLER on their BSA motor cycle.

AFTER SUFFERING A LEG INJURY AT FOOTBALL, Donald Vines of Reybridge is pushed in a wonderful basket invalid chair by Peggy Butler and Eleanor Stevens, who later became his wife. This chair was kept in the vicarage for anyone who was in need of it.

SECTION SIX

Military

DEFENCE TRENCHES being dug during the First World War.

ERNEST CLIFFORD, BORN AT MILLSPLATT, BOX HILL, and his wife, Elizabeth. Ernest served with the Coldstream Guards during the First World War. They lived at Cliff Cottage, Box Hill, at the quarry entrance. Ernest was caretaker at the Moon Aircraft Company, Box Hill.

HERBERT EDWARDS served with the Royal Horse Artillery for ten and a half years and was discharged in 1921. This picture was taken in Egypt. Mr Edwards is standing third from the right.

LEON ARTHAND AT THE WHEEL in India, 1920, while serving with the 1st Battalion Royal Scots.

THIS POSTCARD was written on 5 January 1917 by Walter Ballinger, in France on active service, and received on 6 January by his wife Helen, who lived at Beccle Wood, Biddestone. The message to his family read: 'I received your letter today, that you wrote on December 29th, and am pleased to hear that you are both quite well, as I am. No news today, Love to you both, from your devoted Walter. . .'

WALTER BALLINGER WITH HIS WIFE HELEN and baby Alfred, two years old, prior to leaving for France with the Royal Artillery. Mr Ballinger was at the battle of the Somme. Before joining the army, Walter worked at Stowell Farm, Middlehill, Biddestone, where his family lived.

ALBERT COGSWELL while based at Dover in the Royal Army Medical Corps No. 12 Ambulance Train. During the First World War, the trains transported the wounded around the country in order that they could be dispersed to the various local hospitals.

PERCY WILLIAM BADMINTON who served in the Northumberland Hussars during the First World War, and was killed in action in France on 18 September 1918. With him are his wife Maria and son Cyril.

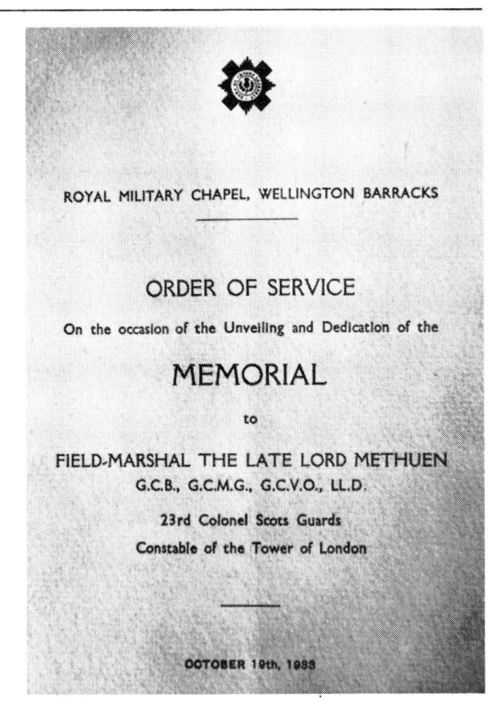

ROYAL MILITARY CHAPEL, WELLINGTON BARRACKS

ORDER OF SERVICE

On the occasion of the Unveiling and Dedication of the

MEMORIAL

to

FIELD-MARSHAL THE LATE LORD METHUEN

G.C.B., G.C.M.G., G.C.V.O., LL.D.

23rd Colonel Scots Guards

Constable of the Tower of London

OCTOBER 19th, 1933

MEMORIAL SERVICE FOR FIELD MARSHALL LORD METHUEN, held in 1933 at the Wellington Barracks. HRH The Prince of Wales was seated very close to the members of Corsham choir who sang at the ceremony. Mr Lewin Spackman was the choirmaster.

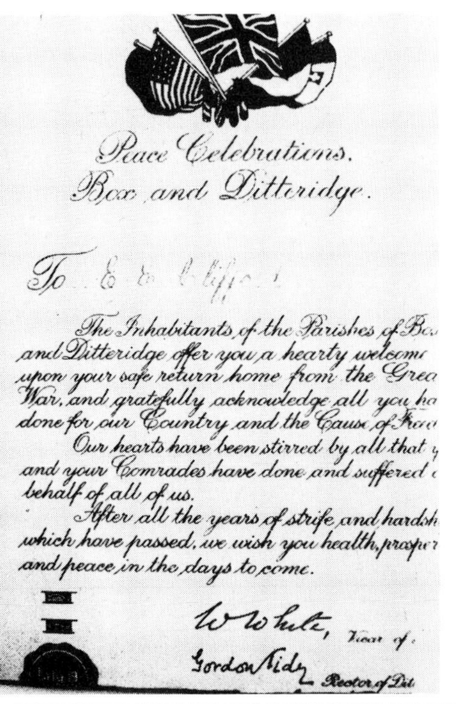

Peace Celebrations.
Box and Ditteridge.

To [illegible]

The Inhabitants of the Parishes of Bo
and Ditteridge offer you a hearty welcom
upon your safe return home from the Grea
War, and gratefully acknowledge all you ha
done for our Country and the Cause of Free
Our hearts have been stirred by all that y
and your Comrades have done and suffered
behalf of all of us.
After all the years of strife and hardsh
which have passed, we wish you health, prosper
and peace in the days to come.

W White, Vicar of
Gordon Kidd, Rector of Dit

THIS CERTIFICATE, awarded to the parishioners of Box who served in the First World War, was dated 1919, but sadly was cut to fit into a photograph frame.

FIELD MARSHALL LORD METHUEN unveiling the new cenotaph at the Park Gates, at the junction of Lacock Road.

CORSHAM PARK GATES AND CENOTAPH with the Park Lodge in the background.

'MACKIE' CURRANT ON HIS ENLISTMENT. 'Mackie' was unfortunately killed on the beaches at Dunkirk aged twenty-one. His home was at Ashley, Box.

DOLLY LODGE, centre, served in the ATS and during her National Service was employed in the cookhouse. She was at both Warminster and Yeovil camps.

MR LEON ARTHAND, fourth from the left, back row, in a photograph taken at the outbreak of the Second World War.

C COMPANY, some of the men of the 5th Wiltshire Regiment, 1841/2, in Kent. Mr Percy Badminton is first left, back row. Colonel Hankey CO, of Stanton St Quintin, and Lieutenant William Fields both died in action.

THE FORERUNNER OF THE HOME GUARD: 262 Protection Company of the Royal Defence Corps. It was renamed in June 1940, at the suggestion of Winston Churchill.

CAD CIVIL DEFENCE TEAM.

CORSHAM TOWN HALL WAS USED AS A CONVALESCENT HOME, and this picture shows the staff ready to receive their patients during the First World War.

CORSHAM COURT was used as a convalescent home for the wounded during the Second World War. Lord and Lady Methuen are shown here with members of the nursing staff and Red Cross drivers. Mrs Christine Currie is standing in the second row, left, in outdoor uniform. Mrs Currie was an ambulance driver throughout the war.

HM QUEEN MARY VISITING THE SICK AND WOUNDED at Corsham Court during the Second World War.

STAFF WHO MANNED THE CONVALESCENT HOSPITAL situated inside Corsham Town Hall attend the presentation ceremony of the motor ambulance by Colonel Spencer. Several of the servicemen recovering from their injuries and illnesses are standing to the left of the picture, their white revers indicate that they are 'war wounded'.

OVER-SEAS LEAGUE

PATRON

HIS MAJESTY THE KING

OVER-SEAS HOUSE. ST. JAMES'S. LONDON. SW1

EMPIRE DAY - 1940

This is to Certify

that EVA CLIFFORD.

HAS HELPED TO PROVIDE COMFORT AND CONTENTMENT TO THE SOLDIERS, SAILORS AND AIRMEN OF THE BRITISH COMMONWEALTH, WHO HAVE RALLIED TO THE CAUSE OF SAFEGUARDING FREEDOM, JUSTICE AND SECURITY.

ALTHOUGH THE WORDING ON THE CERTIFICATE IS A LITTLE AMBIGUOUS, it is in serious heartfelt recognition of the work people did to help the troops during the Second World War.

CORSHAM ATC 1943/4 photographed at Corsham School. Back row, left to right: Des Clifford, -?-, Ron Smith, -?-, Gilbert Smith, Ron Moules. Second row: Ivor Sheppard, David Aust, Herbie Bond, Roy Jackson, Peter Tanner, Pat Tanner. Third row: Albert Bradfield, Ray Brooks, -?-, ? Merrit, Brian Colley, John Daltrey, -?-, Don Abraham, -?-. Seated: -?-, -?-, Bill Gale, -?-, Harry Lakeman, Harold Gale, Bob Allen, -?-, -?-.

THE STAFF OF RUDLOE MANOR. The civilian staff were Kathleen Gingell, ? Osborne, Sheila Lodge, Angela Fenn, Eileen Sproule, Christine Arthand.

RAF RUDLOE MANOR RUGBY TEAM, touring the Channel Islands in 1955. Back row, left to right: -?-, -?-, -?-, -?-, -?-, Snicker, -?-, -?-, Judd (became captain of England in the sixties). Front row: Squirrell, -?-, Langford (Somerset cricketer), Parry, Wing Commander Binks, Ball, -?-.

SECTION SEVEN

Leisure and Sport

DOREEN AND ALISON JONES, winners of the Allotment Competition in 1942.

DOREEN AND ALISON JONES, 1943, second-time winners of the Allotment Competition. They beat 300 men for the title.

LOOKING TOWARDS BOX HILL from the Colerne side of the valley. This picture shows Albert and Florence Cogswell with their son Alec after gathering cowslips. Schoolchildren used to be taken to the fields and Corsham Park to pick cowslips which were made into 'balls', and taken to the hospitals.

PRIMROSING IN WORMCLIFFE LANE, Ashley, Box. Left to right: Ken, Edie and Phyllis Currant, with a holiday friend, Joan, enjoy an activity which, due to legislation banning the picking of wild flowers, cannot be experienced by this and future generations of children.

MRS ARTHAND AND HER DAUGHTERS CHRISTINE AND ANNETTE enjoying a lemonade outside the Station Hotel in the summer of 1939, before the outbreak of war. In the top right-hand corner is the Station Road stoneyard. The large gate was the entrance to the Station Road Glove Factory. Note the Regal Cinema programme board; the Crazy Gang were top of the bill.

TOC H CONCERT FOR THE OVER SIXTIES CLUB. Standing, left to right: Joe James, Mrs Owen, Doreen Jones, Mr Tolley, Glenys Badminton, -?-, -?-, Percy Badminton, Joyce Marsh, Reg Pullen, Cynthia Merrett, Edith Fisher, Mrs Miller, -?-, Jim Mines, Effie Hancock. Sitting: ? Shelton, Dorothy Farmer, -?-, -?-.

DANCERS FROM THE OVER-18S REVUE, 1954. Standing, left to right: Brenda Holden, Clare Boyer, Mabel Godden, Glynis Phillips. Sitting: Alice Skinner, Mary Bennie, Anita Light, Leone Cunningham, Peggy Tanner and Esmé Pavitt.

JOE JAMES AS EVERYMAN, the title role of a medieval Morality play, performed by the Drama Club, 1953.

THE GUARDIAN was the first play in a double bill in Corsham Drama Club's 25th Jubilee year, 1957. The cast, the left to right, were: Joe James, Melanie Bugnius, Peter Henderson, Pamela Arthand, Muriel Sproate and Fred Thomsett.

THE SECOND PLAY during the Jubilee performance was *Androcles and the Lion*. From left to right: -?-, -?-, John Court, Melanie Bugnius, -?-, Jean Hoare, -?-, Pamela Arthand, -?-, -?-, -?-, Queenie Coates, -?-.

RICHARD FOWLER IN HIS SCOUT UNIFORM, with his cousin Frederick Gray, 1917.

BERT PEARCE AND DICK FOWLER, members of Gastard Scouts, carrying far more gear than the scouts of today – note the bush hats, the large scarves, the water bottle and the staves.

THE 1ST CORSHAM BROWNIE PACK ON HOLIDAY AT STOWIE, near Bishop's Sutton. Brown Owl Marion Stevens, is shown enrolling Norma Changty into the Brownies. From the left: June Holloway, Marion Stevens, Carol Masson, Norma Changty, Kathy Fricker, Christine Baker, Denise Bickerstaff. Standing in the front: Jenny Wilson, Lorraine Merrit, Christine Flowerday.

CORSHAM 1ST BROWNIES at Dudsbury Guide Camp, Dorset in 1966. Brown Owl Marion Stevens is front left, with her two daughters, Rebecca and Joanna, on her lap. Mrs Stevens was Brown Owl for twenty-one years.

NESTON RESERVES FOOTBALL TEAM, 1921. Second row, from the left: Stan Sheppard, ? Jones, ? Gale. Front: Fred Hand (centre), Dick Fowler.

CORSHAM LADIES HOCKEY TEAM 1936/7. Back row, left to right: -?-, Edna Grey, Doris Cowley, Nancy Gray, ? King, -?-. Front row: -?-, -?-, ? King, -?-, -?-.

Below right:
H.S. LAKEMAN, IN HIS BOOK *Eighty Years of Cricket, 1848–1928*, tells us that the minute books show how in 1871 'it was felt that "the tent", which had served them until that season, was no longer consistent with the dignity and ambitions of the club. With subscriptions and gifts, a neat little wooden structure with a thatched roof was built.' This picture, taken from Mr Lakeman's book, shows Corsham's 1st Eleven of 1889. Standing, left to right: L. Spackman, C.J. Mayo, A.C. Kinnear, J. Smith, W.G. Allard. Sitting: H.E. Mayo, H. Spackman, W. Spackman, W.H. Robinson. On the ground: C.F. Spackman, S.P. Kinnear.

CORSHAM HOCKEY TEAM, 1936, photographed at Chippenham Sports Ground. Back row, left to right: Percy Badminton, A. White, Reg Pullen, John Paulson, Revd Shaw(?), ? Hughes. Front row: A. Gosnell, W. Holman, A. Fido, H.S. Lakeman, John Norton.

A PEACEFUL AND UNUSUAL VIEW OF CORSHAM CRICKET FIELD, with the pavilion in the far corner. Grove House can just be seen to the left of the pavilion, and the Methuen Arms to the right.

CORSHAM CRICKET GROUND looking toward the warden's house at the Hungerford Almshouses. The building to the right was used by many local organizations for their meetings.

CORSHAM CRICKET CLUB at the presentation of the new scoreboard, 1957. From the left: A. Fido, A. Daniells, F. Lee, G. Daniells, F. White, J. Hall, T. Joy, T. Catt, D. Tilley, T. Wheeler, H. Gale, Col. Masters, Dr Eagles, B. Gale, D. Hazell, K. Boulton, R. Morris, A. St John, N. Way, N. Bence, V. Bence, V. Pearce, J. Newman, G. Reeves, B. Woodham, R. Hopkins, H. Baines.

BOX CRICKET CLUB, 1913. Standing left to right: W. Bradfield, E. Southard, B. Vezey, S. McIlwraith (Capt.), H. Benjamin, V. Southard, R.S. Ponting, H. Milsom. Sitting: J. Bradfield, G. Hale, R. Shewring, W.S. Bascombe, A. Bradfield.

BOX CRICKET CLUB, 1936/7. Standing, left to right: George Hinton, Jack Gee, Jack Tottle, Ben Veasey, Ivor Ball, Arthur Stevens, Bill Guy, Mr Pepper. Sitting: -?-, -?-, -?-, Stan Brunt, Os Butt, ? Gape (scorer), Alec Cogswell.

CRICKET CLUB DINNER at the Queen's Head, Box. Sitting, left to right: Geoff Bence, -?-, Stan Burrows, -?-, Phil Lambert, Nigel Bence, Cecil Lambert, -?-, Walter Brown, Alec Benjamin, -?-, Peter Odey, Herbie Benjamin, Fred Sandell, -?-, -?-, -?-, H.H. Sawyer (in far corner), -?-, Tom Bence, visiting Vice Presidents. Standing: -?-, -?-, -?-, -?-, Leslie Bence, Brian Weekes, Ken Boulton, Peter Milsom, -?-, Len Weekes, John Tottle.

SECTION EIGHT

Occasions

PICKWICK ROAD, decorated for the celebrations of the coming of age of the Hon. Paul A. Methuen, in 1907.

THE 1ST CORSHAM SCOUTS ACTIVITY EVENT in Corsham Park, 1950. With the Hon. John Methuen, second from the right, on the platform are: David Stevens, Ken Oatley, Peter Hudson, Tony Wilkins and Derek Farleigh.

THIS MEETING OF THE WOMEN'S SUFFRAGE PILGRIMAGE was held at Corsham Town Hall on 16 July 1913. The notice attached to the vehicle in the background reads 'Lands End to London Women's Suffrage Societies'.

CORSHAM TOWN BAND, founded in 1888, leading a procession of children past the Methodist church in Pickwick Road.

SOME OF THE PEOPLE TAKING PART IN THE MAY FESTIVAL, 1938. From the left (as nearly as possible!): Mrs Davis, Mr Bryant, Mrs Pullen, -?-, Mrs Smith, Edna and Dorothy Dobson, Audrey Reed, Jean Batley, Doreen Jones, Joyce Pullen, Joan Davis, Audrey Davis, Olive Reed, Jean Davis, Joan James, Anne and Ruth Jones, Hadyn Brooks, Beatrice Salter, Diana Smith, Janet Gale, ? Coulson, ? Smith, Brian Ludlow, Mr Farmer. The colour scheme for the tableau was blue, mauve and green.

CONGREGATIONAL CHURCH FESTIVAL, May 1938. The maids-in-waiting to the May Queen, all wearing white dresses, are, from left to right: Dorothy Dobson, Edna Dobson, Doreen Jones, Ivy Ludlow, Phyllis Shillater, Dora ?.

A TOC H OUTING TO OXFORD, 1944. Back row, left to right: -?-, Bernard Tattersfield, Doreen and Alison Jones, Mrs Aust. Next row: Joan Tucker, Glenys Badminton, -?-. Next row: Dorothy Farmer, Mrs Owen, Mrs Hancock, Mrs John, Mrs Barnett, -?-, -?-, -?-, -?-, -?-, -?-, -?-, Amy Miller, Monica Barnett, Hazel Shenton.

THE CONSERVATIVE ASSOCIATION CELEBRATION PARTY at the end of the Second World War. Back row, left to right: -?-, -?-, Len Love, -?-, Mrs Bateman, Mrs Gale, -?-, -?-. Next row: -?-, -?-, -?-, -?-, Raymond Smith, Tommy Swailes, Reg Stainer, Norman McMillan, Mr Bateman, Mr Head, Mr Maskell, -?-, -?-, Bill Gale, -?-, Mr Munnery, -?-, -?-, Edward Jones. Front row, standing: -?-, -?-, Mrs Swailes, -?-, -?-, Mrs Masell, Mrs Salter, -?-, -?-, Mrs Head, Mrs Stainer, Mrs Pritchard, -?-, Mrs Munnery, Mrs Jones.

MEMBERS OF THE ROYAL ANTEDILUVIAN ORDER OF BUFFALOES LODGE, Corsham, on parade on Armistice Day, soon after the end of the Second World War. Mr Bill Gale is on the right-hand side, rear rank. The Girl Guide on the left was the daughter of Jack Snell, the blacksmith, of Pickwick Road.

THE CHRISTMAS PARTY AT MISS BAILEY'S SCHOOL in the High Street in 1943. Adults, left to right: -?-, Mr Bailey, -?-, -?-, -?-, -?-, Poppy Bailey. Children, from the back row, left to right: Stella Carter, Malcolm Farleigh, Joy Howell, Richard Todd, Marion Farleigh, John Brown, -?-, June Marsh, Richard Bebbington, Valerie Jacobs, Derek Woods, Max Salmon, -?-, Maurice Cload, -?-, Mrs Bibbington, -?-, -?-, Irene Taylor, Pat Woods. Front row: Monica and Mary ?. Centre: Miss Bailey, -?-, Trevor Payne, John Cook.

SECONDARY MODERN SCHOOL SPORTS DAY, 1959. Seated left to right: Michael James, Clive Thomas and Len Thomas.

A PROGRAMME of events held to celebrate the Coronation of Queen Elizabeth II.

A STREET PARTY to celebrate the coronation of Queen Elizabeth II, Clutterbuck Road, shows the pre-fabricated bungalows which were built for war workers and evacuated families during the Second World War. These bungalows have been replaced by the Secondary Modern School. Left-hand side of table: Allan Shevlen, -?-, Margaret Shevlin, Anne Hulbert, Jackie Speares, Jean Thomas, Marlene Lockyer, Nellie Thomas, Lil Speares, Daisy Lockyer, -?-, Mrs Shevlin. Right-hand side: -?-, -?-, -?-, Jock Speares, Len Thomas, Lillian Warman, Eileen Lockyer, George Lockyer, Bet Moore. Children at bottom table: -?-, -?-, Eileen Sculley, Jane Moore, Richard Thomas, Hilary Speares.

SIR SEYMOUR HOWARD OF COURTLANDS, Lacock Road, Lord Mayor of London, 1954, at the Mansion House greeting Winston Churchill and Mrs Churchill. Mrs M. Eagles and her sister Mrs J. Weaver were Matrons of Honour and are standing behind the mayoral chair.

DR AND MRS EAGLES, with Mrs J. Weaver, on the balcony of the Mansion House, watching the arrival of Sir Seymour Howard's Lord Mayor's Show procession in 1954.

A REUNION DINNER at Bath of retired engineers from the CAD, Corsham, on the day that President John Kennedy was assassinated in 1963. Mr Vines is seventh from the right, centre back row.

LEADING MARSHFIELD TOWN BAND past Ben Drew's bakery in Devizes Road, Box are, from the left, the Revd Malting; John Brook, Chairman of Calne and Chippenham Rural District Council and of the Box Parish Council; Bert Cogswell, Secretary of Oddfellows; Mr Hayward, Secretary of RAOB.

THE LAYING OF THE FOUNDATION STONE in 1907 of the Methodist Church Hall. The church building can just be seen to the right of the picture.

ONE OF THE ANNUAL CHRISTMAS PARTIES held at the Rising Sun, before it was destroyed by a fearful gas explosion in 1957. All the children from Box Hill were invited to these parties every year. Maureen and Malcolm Pashley are to the right of centre in the front.

BOX CHURCH HARVEST SUPPER, 1956 or 1957. Left to right: Revd Selwyn Smith, Mrs Esther Swift, Mrs Beatrice Toogood, Miss Anna Grayson, Mrs Betty Beavan, Miss Eva Clifford, Mrs Joan Wynne, Mrs Daniels and her daughter.

AN OUTING TO LONGLEAT FROM GASTARD in 1937, organized by the football club. From left to right: Leonard Thomas, George Merritt, Bill Weston, Bert Porter, Fred Gray.

VE DAY PEACE CELEBRATIONS AT GASTARD at the end of the Second World War. This fancy dress parade processed through the village led by John Bull, Mr Thake. Don Aust is standing in the gateway.

NESTON PARK IS TWO MILES FROM CORSHAM and is the home of the Fuller family.

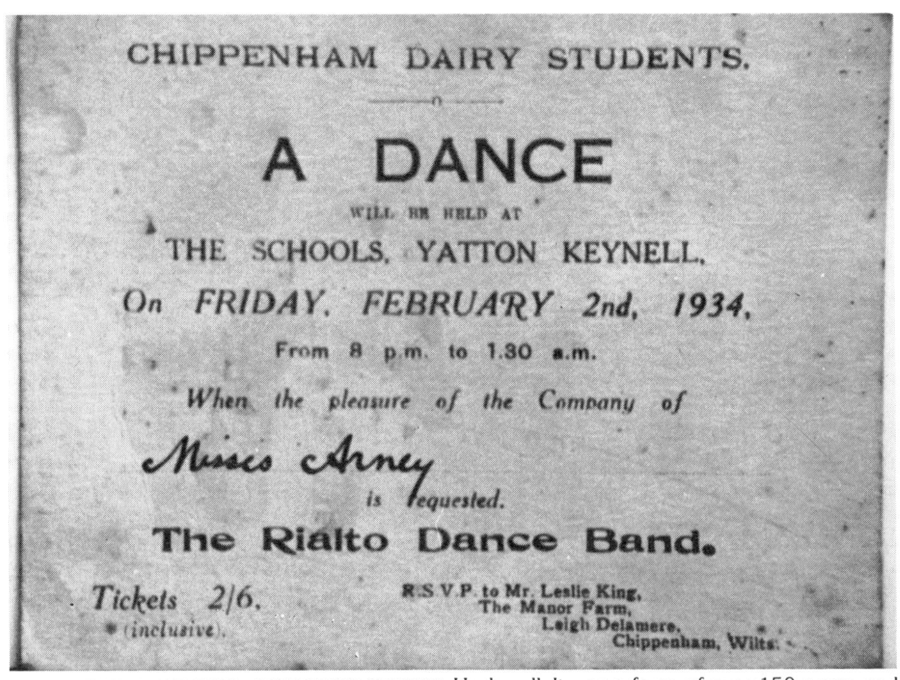
CHIPPENHAM DAIRY STUDENTS.

A DANCE

WILL BE HELD AT

THE SCHOOLS, YATTON KEYNELL,

On *FRIDAY, FEBRUARY 2nd, 1934,*

From 8 p.m. to 1.30 a.m.

When the pleasure of the Company of

Misses Arney

is requested.

The Rialto Dance Band.

Tickets 2/6.
(inclusive).

R.S.V.P. to Mr. Leslie King,
The Manor Farm,
Leigh Delamere,
Chippenham, Wilts.

THE ARNEY FAMILY FARMED AT POCKERIDGE FARM, Hudswell. It was a farm of over 150 acres and William George Arney was in residence in 1935.

SECTION NINE

Locations

AN AERIAL VIEW OF CORSHAM, just after the war, showing the High Street carving its way between the many different types of buildings that go to make Corsham such an interesting town. Now there is a large modern shopping precinct behind the buildings in the near left corner, and the gardens, front right, are a car park. This picture was taken before the houses were built in Bences Lane, to which the fields in the upper left corner testify.

CORSHAM HIGH STREET from the Pickwick Road end. Note the wonderful awning over James's hardware shop on the left. This photograph also predates Cawte's movement into the up and coming automotive business.

AN OLD ENGRAVING OF CORSHAM COURT.

CORSHAM COURT, THE HOME OF LORD JOHN METHUEN. It was completed in 1582 by Customer Smythe, with parts later remodelled by Nash. In the seventeenth century Corsham House belonged to the Hungerfords of Farleigh but it passed to the Methuen family in 1742.

THE JUNCTION OF THE HIGH STREET WITH PRIORY STREET, which is marked by the Mayo fountain. The clock on the Town Hall, on the right, is mounted over a medallion portrait of HM Queen Victoria. It was erected in 1897 to commemorate Her Majesty's Diamond Jubilee.

THE FLEMISH BUILDINGS, Corsham, built in the sixteenth century for the Huguenot weavers who fled their country in 1685 because of religious persecution. The upper storeys of the large house next door to the post office are thought to have been stores for the woven woollen cloth.

A VIEW OF PICKWICK ROAD with the White Lion public house just visible on the left-hand side.

SEALEY'S UNDERTAKING BUSINESS, which offers a twenty-four hour service, nearly hides Corsham's first fish and chip shop (the little shed in the middle of the picture). To the left of Sealey's was the Regal Cinema, and at the end of the programme the audience would rush to leave the cinema and get into the queue for a hot supper.

LACOCK ROAD, taken from the Lodge, showing the almshouses. A beautiful gallery runs the length of this wing of the house on the top floor, and beneath it are the little houses built for the poor of the parish by Lord and Lady Hungerford in 1668.

PRIORY STREET, showing the row of elegant houses to the right, and the Baptist chapel to the left. In 1903 there were three Baptist chapels in the Corsham area.

THE FRONT PORCH AT THE WARDEN'S HOUSE, with the coat of arms of the Hungerford family, who endowed it, and the almshouses attached. The room behind the magnificent topiary peacock was the classroom. The seats and pulpit were still in existence in the room in 1970. The peacock and the beautiful espalier pear tree on the side of the house were cut down at the end of the 1960s when the gardens were 'tidied up'!

THIS PAINTING OF CORSHAM PARK GATES, showing the Lodge to the left, was presented to Mr William Badminton when he was licensee of the White Lion. The Badminton family lived in the Park Lodge for some while, before the First World War.

POUND PILL FROM THE RAILWAY BRIDGE, looking toward Corsham, before the houses were built in the field on the left-hand side, where the telephone poles are situated. The Pound, an enclosure for animals found straying or awaiting collection, was almost on the site of the Bowling Club pavilion.

THE CROSS KEYS INN on the Bristol to London Road (A4). The small house in the centre of the picture used to be the old Fever House or Pest House as it was called. It was demolished in the late 1960s.

THE GWR LINE BETWEEN LONDON AND BRISTOL, 120 miles long, was opened in 1841. Corsham station boasted a neat little hotel, which was demolished when the station was purchased by Hancocks, the coal merchants.

POTLEY LANE, FROM THE RAILWAY BRIDGE. These houses were completed as the war began in 1939/40. To the left of the road can be seen the trackway, used by the stone companies to transport the blocks of stone to the wharf.

THIS PEACEFUL SCENE WITH ITS OLD-FASHIONED IRON LAMP-POST was taken at Potley Lane in 1939 (now called Pockeridge Road). This cluster of new houses had an unfortunate start. As they were completed, war broke out, and a wide cross section of local people and evacuated families were thrown together. Also the surrounding fields were built over to provide accommodation for troops. The encampments were built by an army of Irishmen, many of whom were billeted in the houses. Some stayed and married local girls. During the course of the war Royal Marines, American troops and Tank Corps Divisions were all housed in these camps. The wall of Potley railway bridge was knocked down many times by tanks misjudging the corner.

POCKERIDGE HOUSE was home of the Yockneys, a quarry owning family, before becoming the RAOC Officers' Mess. There is a story that an ancestor of the family, a young lady, threw herself off Box Tunnel, just across the lane from the garden, and now haunts the house.

POCKERIDGE COTTAGE, HUDSWELL. This house was used as the Medical Inspection Rooms during the war. Note the line of an archway around the window on the far left. This was where a corridor was fitted, which connected the surgery with the wooden hutment used as a ward, to the left of the cottage. Once a new medical unit had been erected nearer to Basil Hill Barracks, the cottage was used as the Mess Steward's house, and the ward became a billet for the soldiers who staffed the Officers' Mess. This was later converted into a bungalow for Mr A. Hinton, the head groundsman.

LINLEYS, A SMALL HAMLET BETWEEN CORSHAM AND GASTARD. The nearby Claremont House was once a private school. During the Second World War it was a school for evacuated children. It is now a residential home for the elderly.

IN THE DOMESDAY SURVEY, the owner of Hazelbury Manor was named as 'Croc the Huntsman', and the Royal Forests were his responsibility. In more recent years it was a girls' school, but is now a private residence again.

THE CHEQUERS PUBLIC HOUSE, Box, the residence of Mr Vezey, where Box Cricket Club was formed in 1864.

HAZLEBURY HILL, Box, showing Hazelbury Cottage.

A VERY PEACEFUL VIEW OF BOX showing how the village curves around the hillside.

THE FIRE BRIGADE in attendance sorting through the debris of the Rising Sun public house, Box, after the explosion caused by a gas leak, which demolished the building and killed three people on Tuesday 3 December 1957: the licensee Bill Griffin, his wife Joyce and their four-year-old son Andrew. The only survivor was their daughter Jane.

LOOKING FROM ASHLEY FARM TOWARDS BOX with the cemetery chapel in the middle distance; the burial ground is much enlarged now. The cemetery was formed in 1858.

HARTHAM HOUSE was built by James Wyatt, 1790–5, but has had several additons.

THIS 'CHAPEL', was built in the grounds of Hartham House in 1862 and designed by P.C. Hardwick. It is described as 'quite big'. It is in the Perpendicular style and has a north-west tower.

WESTWELLS FARM. True to its name, during hot summer seasons, there was always water in the wells and many times villagers were supplied from these wells whenever there was a water shortage.

GASTARD HOUSE, which was the seat of Miss J.E. Fowler. This home has now been converted into flats.

MR AND MRS SHEPPARD lived at this house in Neston, at 13 Elley Green.

JAGGARDS HOUSE, the seat of the Fuller family at Neston.

EASTON FARM AND GARDEN. The older wing, on the right, has concave mullions at the windows, and there was a cheese room and a brew house for ale. There were three sixty-gallon barrels in the brew house, in which the ale matured. There would be three 'mashings': the first mashing was for the house, the second went to pay the farmworkers, and the third, the weakest brew, was given to the men when working in the fields. The tun dish (funnel) guided the best ale through the alehouse floor straight into the house barrels in the cellar. The ale boy always had to whistle when carrying the jugs of ale so that the farmer knew that he was not having a crafty sip!

THE TOLL-HOUSE, Atworth, beside the Devizes to Bath road.

WADSWICK FARM, at Upper Wadswick, Box, a farm of about 300 acres, was rented by Mr Hazel in around 1946; prior to that the farmer had been a Mr Bird. It is no longer a farm. Note the handcart for conveying the milk churns to and from the milking parlour. The Churns were left at the gate for collection by the Milk Marketing Board.

ACKNOWLEDGEMENTS

Mrs P. Alford • Mrs E. Anderson • Mr & Mrs Badminton • Mrs & Mrs I. Ball
Mr A. Ballinger • Mrs E. Brown • Mr & Mrs A. Carter • Mr A. Cogswell
Dr & Mrs Eagles • Mrs R. Edwards • Mrs V. Fowler •
Mr Hampton • Mr C. Hancock • Mr Hathaway • Mr J. James • Miss A. Jones
Miss D. Jones • Mr B. Little • Miss D. Lodge • Mrs Martin
Mrs P. Matthews • Mr & Mrs Munnery • Mrs Northover • Mrs Pashley
Mr Powell • Mrs Reid • Mrs Rodgers •Miss E. Rossiter
Mrs W. Sheppard • Mrs E. Slade • Mr & Mrs J. Stannard
Mrs M. Stevens • Mr & Mrs D. Squirrell • Mr & Mrs G. Stoneman-Merret
Mr P. Tanner • Mr J.M. Taylor • Mr & Mrs L. Thomas • Mrs Turner
Mr M.Turner • Mrs A. Wilson • Mr M. Wilson • Mr P. Wilson.

Most of the postcards used are attributable to Mr H. Spackman or Mr W. Hardwell.